MONEYWISE

MANAGING MONEY

Nancy Dickmann

BROWN BEAR BOOKS

Published by Brown Bear Books Ltd
4877 N. Circulo Bujia
Tucson, AZ 85718
USA

and

Studio G14, Regent Studios,
1 Thane Villas, London N7 7PH, UK

ISBN 978-1-78121-928-7 (library bound)
ISBN 978-1-78121-934-8 (paperback)

Library of Congress Cataloging-in-Publication Data available on request

Text: Nancy Dickmann
Designer: Trudi Webb
Design Manager: Keith Davis
Children's Publisher: Anne O'Daly

Manufactured in the United States of America
CPSIA compliance information: Batch#AG/PO 5656

Picture Credits
The photographs in this book are used by permission and through the courtesy of:

Cover: Keith Davis; Interior: Shutterstock: Iakov Filimonov 10, Monkey Business Images 6-7, 12-13, 16-17, 18-19, 20-21, Odua Images 9, PeopleImages.com 4, Tonovi Zamrznuti 15.

All other artwork and photography
© Brown Bear Books.

t-top, r-right, l-left, c-center, b-bottom

Brown Bear Books has made every attempt to contact the copyright holder. If you have any information about omissions please contact:
licensing@brownbearbooks.co.uk

Websites
The website addresses in this book were valid at the time of going to press. However, it is possible that contents or addresses may change following publication of this book. No responsibility for any such changes can be accepted by the author or the publisher. Readers should be supervised when they access the Internet.

Words in **bold** appear in the Words to Know on page 23

Contents

What's in Your WALLET?

Having a bit of money is a nice feeling. Where do you get yours?

Some children get an **allowance** every week. Maybe you earn money for doing jobs around the house. You might fold laundry or load the dishwasher. You might get money as a present on your birthday. Any money that you receive is called income.

Doing chores at home helps your family. It also teaches you responsibility.

Income for Adults

Grownups have income, too. It often comes from a job. They get paid in return for the work they do. There are other kinds of income. Grownups might get money from the government, such as **welfare**. They might get child support or other money from a family member.

Many grownups' income is a mix of different types. Some grownups get money for renting out property.

Spending MONEY

What do you like to spend your money on?

Income is the money that you receive. **Expenses** are the money that you spend. Some expenses are about the same each week or month. Others don't follow a pattern.

You might decide to buy a new book. You might buy a movie ticket as a treat.

You might have regular expenses, such as dues for a club you belong to.

Monthly Expenses

Grownups spend money on things like **rent** and food. They pay for electricity and gas. These usually cost about the same each month. Many people also spend on other things, such as birthday presents, new clothes, or eating out. These amounts change from month to month.

MONEY TIP

Keep a spending diary for a month. Write down everything you spend money on. Was it more or less than you expected?

Finding a BALANCE

What's the key to managing money? It's all about balance!

Take a period of time, such as a month. Figure out how much **income** you'll have from allowance or jobs. Now think about what you want to buy. You can only spend the money you have. You'll need to balance the money coming in and the money going out.

MONEY QUESTION

If you borrow money, you have to pay it back later. Do you think it's better to try to save money by cutting back on what you spend?

Spending Too Much

If you try to spend more than your income, you'll run out of money. Sometimes this happens to grownups. Then they need to earn more, or cut back on their spending. Sometimes they end up borrowing money to cover their expenses.

It's a good idea to write down a plan for how you want to spend your money.

Something LEFT OVER

Do you spend your money or save some for later?

If income and expenses were perfectly balanced, then you'd finish each month with nothing left over. In real life, they're usually a bit different. Try to spend less than your income. That way, there's always a bit of money left over. You can save up for the future.

Part of managing your money is making good choices about how you spend it.

MONEY TIP

Some expenses aren't a surprise, but they only happen once or twice a year. This includes things like vacations or birthday parties.

Just in Case

We can't predict every expense. Maybe a pet gets sick. Or you lose your umbrella and need to buy a new one. Maybe your oven stops working and needs to be repaired. Expenses like these can come as a surprise. You should always have a little extra money—just in case.

Saving for THE FUTURE

Managing your money well can give you a brighter future.

Taking care of your money isn't just about deciding how to spend it. It's also about deciding how to save it. Many people try to save for the future if they can. Putting some of your money into savings should be part of every spending plan.

Parents and grandparents often save money for a child's future.

Why Save?

Many people save money to pay for college. Getting a degree can be expensive. They might save to buy a house or start a business. Many people also save for when they retire. Once they stop working, they'll use the money they saved to pay for their expenses.

MONEY TIP

It might feel like these kinds of decisions are a long way in the future. But the sooner you start saving, the more money you'll have.

Bank ACCOUNTS

Where do you keep your money?

Some people keep their money in a piggy bank or a special box. Grownups often keep their money in a **bank account**. The bank takes care of the money until you need it. You can add money to your bank account whenever you want. You can also take it out.

Using Your Money

You can go to the bank to get **cash** from your account. With some kinds of accounts, you can also use a card to spend at a store. The bank keeps track of how much money is in your bank account. It keeps it safe from being lost or stolen.

A bank often sends a **statement** every month. It shows how much money you put into your account, and how much you took out.

You can use a card at an **ATM** to get money from your bank account.

Making a BUDGET

To manage your money, you need a budget.

A **budget** is a plan for your money. It covers a period of time, such as a month or a year. The budget has an **estimate** of how much income you will have. A budget lists what you plan to spend it on and how much you plan to save. It shows how much you will have left over at the end.

A budget doesn't only plan spending. It can include savings plans, too. How much money will you put aside each month?

Close Enough?

A budget is never exact. You can only estimate what things will cost. They might end up costing more or less. There might be expenses you didn't plan for. That's why people often plan to have money left over.

You can make a budget for a single project, like planning a party.

Sticking TO IT

Making a budget is just the first step. You have to stick to it!

Have your plans ever changed? Maybe you and your friend planned to go for a bike ride, but then decided to play video games instead. Spending plans can change, too. But a budget only works if you stick to your plan as closely as you can.

You don't always have to spend money to have fun. Some kinds of fun are free!

MONEY QUESTION

Some people set aside money in their budget for treats. Do you think that sticking to a budget is easier if you can still have a few treats?

Temptation

What if you're out playing and an ice cream truck drives past? Ice cream wasn't in your budget, but it's a hot day and you really want one. If you buy one now, you might not have enough for the t-shirt you want. Is it worth it?

SPLIT It Up!

One way to budget is to split your money into three "pots."

Many adults budget using the 50-30-20 plan. Fifty percent of their money goes on **needs**, such as rent and food. Thirty percent goes on **wants**, such as restaurant meals and day trips. The other twenty percent goes into savings.

Wants are things that are nice to have, but that you could live without.

Use the spend pot for candy.

Spend, Save, Share!

Could you divide your money in three? Use part of it for spending on things that you want. Save up the second part for the future or for a big purchase. The third part is for sharing—giving to charity or spending on gifts for others.

Use the share pot for presents.

Use the save pot for a new bike.

MONEY QUESTION

How you split the money between your three pots is up to you. How much will you put in each? Which will be the biggest?

Use Your Skills!

It's time to test out your money knowledge!
You can check your answers on page 24.

1 Noah gets an allowance of $5 per week. He wants to buy a football shirt that costs $20. How long will it take him to save up?

2 Aisha is making a budget for a birthday party. She has $60 to spend. She wants to spend $30 on food, $20 on decorations, and $15 on party bags. Will she have enough?

3 How can you get money out of your bank account?

Find out More

Websites

coolkidfacts.com/money-for-kids/

ducksters.com/money/budgeting_money.php

investopedia.com/personal-finance/10-tips-teach-your-child-save/

Books

Gaertner, Meg. **Spending and Saving Money** (Community Economics). North Mankato, Minn.: Cody Koala, 2019.

Hardyman, Robyn. **Money, Goals and Budgeting** (Money Skills for Kids). New York: Rosen Publishing, 2018.

Sherman, Jill. **Money: What You Need to Know.** Mankato, Minn.: Capstone Press, 2018.

Words to Know

allowance money that some parents regularly give their children, often as a reward for good behavior or helping out

ATM a machine that works like a mini bank, letting people take cash out of their account

bank account an arrangement with a bank so that they can take care of your money

budget a plan showing how much money you expect to have and how you will spend it

cash money in the form of coins or paper notes

estimate a rough guess based on the information you have

expenses things that must be paid for, such as food or rent

income the amount of money you get from earnings or other sources

needs the basic essentials that a person needs to survive, such as food and shelter

rent a monthly fee paid to live in a house or apartment

statement a document that shows all the money going in or out of a bank account

wants thinks that people enjoy having but don't actually need to survive

welfare money paid by the government to people who need it to live

Index

Answers

1. Noah will have saved up enough in four weeks, as long as he doesn't spend his allowance on anything else.
2. Aisha doesn't have enough money. Her costs add up to $65, so she will need to spend less.
3. You can go to a bank to take cash out, or use a card at an ATM.